AMERICAN CITIZENSHIP

CONSTITUT
RIGHTS

by Jill Sherman

Content Consultant
Richard Bell
Associate Professor, Department of History
University of Maryland

Core Library

An Imprint of Abdo Publishing
abdopublishing.com

abdopublishing.com

Published by Abdo Publishing, a division of ABDO, PO Box 398166, Minneapolis, Minnesota 55439. Copyright © 2017 by Abdo Consulting Group, Inc. International copyrights reserved in all countries. No part of this book may be reproduced in any form without written permission from the publisher. Core Library™ is a trademark and logo of Abdo Publishing.

Printed in the United States of America, North Mankato, Minnesota
042016
092016

THIS BOOK CONTAINS
RECYCLED MATERIALS

Cover Photo: Albin Lohr-Jones/SIPA USA/AP Images
Interior Photos: Albin Lohr-Jones/SIPA USA/AP Images, 1; Universal History Archive/UIG/Getty Images, 4; GraphicaArtis/Getty Images, 8, 43; Chip Somodevilla/Getty Images, 10, 45; Mandel Ngan/AFP/Getty Images, 12; Jewel Samad/Getty Images, 18, 30; John Locher/AP Images, 20; Damian Dovarganes/AP Images, 24; Red Line Editorial, 34, 41; Eric Risberg/AP Images, 35; Paul Schutzer/The LIFE Picture Collection/Getty Images, 36

Editor: Sharon F. Doorasamy
Series Designer: Laura Polzin

Cataloging-in-Publication Data
Names: Sherman, Jill, author.
Title: Constitutional rights / by Jill Sherman.
Description: Minneapolis, MN : Abdo Publishing, [2017] | Series: American
    citizenship | Includes bibliographical references and index.
Identifiers: LCCN 2015960484 | ISBN 9781680782417 (lib. bdg.) |
    ISBN 9781680776522 (ebook)
Subjects: LCSH: United States. Constitution--Juvenile literature. | Constitutional history--United States--Juvenile literature.
Classification: DDC 973.3--dc23
LC record available at http://lccn.loc.gov/2015960484

CONTENTS

CHAPTER ONE

THE MAKING OF THE US CONSTITUTION

T he American Revolution (1775–1783) ended after an eight-year war. Thirteen American colonies won their independence from Britain. The American colonists then established the United States of America. Independence brought new struggles. Now the leaders needed to create a new government.

General George Washington led the American colonies to victory over Britain.

A group known as the Continental Congress developed the Articles of Confederation. These articles established the new nation's first government. The articles had weaknesses, though. They gave the Congress no power to raise money to pay its debts. The Articles gave power to the states rather than a central government. This led to problems. The Congress could not force the states to obey its laws. It could not create an army. The nation's leaders realized the United States needed a stronger national government to survive.

The Constitutional Convention

Delegates from 12 of the 13 states met in the summer of 1787. They gathered in Philadelphia, Pennsylvania. The meeting was called the Constitutional Convention. The delegates planned to make changes to the Articles of Confederation. They ended up writing an entirely new document.

The delegates discussed ideas throughout the summer. They needed to figure out how the new government would work. Heated debates erupted. Eventually the delegates reached compromises. They created the US Constitution. The Constitution spells out how the United States is to be run. George Washington was the first to sign the document. Of the 55 delegates, 39 signed. Each state had to ratify the Constitution before it became law.

The Anti-Federalists

The Constitution set up a strong central government. Supporters of the document called themselves Federalists. Critics became known as anti-Federalists. They

PERSPECTIVES
Limiting Power

Virginia delegate George Mason believed strongly in individual freedom and states' rights. He criticized early drafts of the Constitution. He thought that it gave the federal government too much power. He suggested starting the Constitution with a bill of rights. His idea was defeated. As a result, Mason refused to sign the completed document. But his influence was clear. The Bill of Rights later became part of the Constitution. Mason is often called the Father of the Bill of Rights.

Howard Chandler Christy's 1940 painting of the signing of the US Constitution hangs in the US Capitol.

believed the Constitution did not do enough to protect individual rights. These rights include freedom of speech, religion, and the press. They also believed that the state governments needed more control.

Delegate James Madison realized the need for a compromise. He drafted changes to the Constitution. He included ideas from Federalists and anti-Federalists. The first ten amendments became known as the Bill of Rights. The states ratified the Bill of Rights by 1791.

The Federalist Papers

James Madison, Alexander Hamilton, and John Jay wrote a series of 85 essays encouraging the states to ratify the new Constitution. These writings are known as the Federalist papers. They were published in 1787 and 1788. In the essays, the authors criticize the Articles of Confederation and argue that the country needs a strong central government. They explain that a federal government gives the nation the best chance to preserve justice, stability, and personal liberty.

An activist exercises her right to free speech and to protest against the government during a demonstration in Washington, DC.

American Rights and Liberties

The Bill of Rights stands as a powerful symbol of individual liberty. It has stood the test of time. It still protects basic freedoms in the United States. Americans can speak freely. They have the right to fair trials. They can worship however they want. These rights are as important today as they were in 1791.

The US Constitution went through many changes as it was being drafted. The final version begins with the words "We the People." This introduction, or preamble, explains that the power of government belongs to the American people:

> We the people of the United States, in order to form a more perfect union, establish justice, insure domestic tranquility, provide for the common defense, promote the general welfare, and secure the blessings of liberty to ourselves and our posterity, do ordain and establish this Constitution for the United States of America.

Source: "Two Versions of the Preamble to the Constitution, 1787." www.gilderlehrman.org. The Gilder Lehrman Institute of American History, n.d. Web. Accessed January 31, 2016.

Consider Your Audience

Review the preamble carefully. Adapt this passage for your parents or school friends. Write a blog post about it for them. Write it so it can be understood by them. How does your new approach differ from the original text, and why?

FREEDOM OF RELIGION AND SPEECH

The United States had declared its independence from a harsh British government. The new nation's citizens valued personal freedoms. The writers of the Constitution and the Bill of Rights agreed.

The First Amendment to the US Constitution includes several key freedoms. The first two are freedom of religion and speech. Another is the

A Girl Scout color guard carries the US flag before an address by President Barack Obama at the Islamic Society in Maryland on February 3, 2016.

Freedom to Assemble and Petition

Under the First Amendment, Americans have the right to gather in groups. The government is not supposed to interfere. Gathering together can give individual citizens more power than they would have alone. They can show a united front. They can better share their ideas and create change. Petitioning the government gives people a way to bring issues to their leaders' attention.

right to peacefully assemble. Citizens can gather together to express their ideas. This includes protests against the government. The amendment also spells out a related right. It is the right to petition the government. This means citizens can express their views to government officials. They can argue for or against laws.

Some early Americans had fled Britain to escape religious persecution. The Pilgrims sailed across the Atlantic on the *Mayflower* in 1620. They rejected the Church of England. The Puritans came later, in 1630. They supported the

Church of England. But they wanted to reform the Church. The Founding Fathers wanted Americans to worship however they chose. They also agreed that the government should not pass laws to favor a religion.

Equally important was freedom of speech. Colonists had been punished for speaking against Britain's king. The Founding Fathers wanted American citizens to be able to speak freely. This included the freedom to criticize the government.

The right of free speech extends to the press. The government

PERSPECTIVES
The Right to Say It

The French writer Voltaire often spoke about free speech. He was well known for his wit. He is sometimes credited with a famous quote about free speech. The quote is "I disapprove of what you say, but I will defend to the death your right to say it." The statement highlights the importance of free speech. But the quote is not his. The words belong to English writer Evelyn Beatrice Hall. She wrote them while summarizing Voltaire's views on free speech.

does not control what Americans read. Writers and reporters can report as they choose. They can share their opinions with the public. Citizens might never learn about government mistakes if not for this freedom. Well-informed citizens are essential to democracy.

Limitations of Free Speech

The First Amendment does not protect all kinds of speech. It is illegal to falsely yell "fire" in a crowded theater. Doing this would create panic. People could be injured as they tried to escape.

Similarly, the Constitution does not protect false or damaging statements. They could hurt a person or business's reputation. Making a spoken statement such as this is slander. If printed, it is called libel.

In schools, free speech is also limited. School officials may decide what is appropriate for their students. They may deny a student permission to print an article in the school newspaper. They might punish students who use crude language at school events.

Preventing people from speaking freely is called censorship. It can affect newspapers, books, speeches, music, and art. It can even mean blocking websites. People may ask for books to be removed from libraries. The government has decided that certain words cannot be said on broadcast television or radio. Americans have the right to push back against limitations on free speech. They can fight censorship in the courts to defend their First Amendment rights.

FURTHER EVIDENCE

Chapter Two talks about the First Amendment right to free speech. What is one of the chapter's main points? What evidence is included to support this point? Go to the website below. Find a quote that supports the right of free speech. Does the quote on the website support the main point? Does it present new evidence?

Banned and Challenged Books
mycorelibrary.com/constitutional-rights

CHAPTER THREE

RIGHT TO BEAR ARMS

The Second Amendment states that Americans have the right to own guns. The American Revolution was a factor in the Founding Fathers' decision to write this amendment. The colonies lacked an army when the revolution began. Instead, groups of men joined together to form local fighting groups

Demonstrators in the nation's capital protest in support of the Second Amendment right to bear arms.

A woman looks at a handgun at the Shooting, Hunting, and Outdoor Trade Show in Las Vegas, Nevada, in January 2016.

called militias. They used their own weapons. The militias played a crucial role in defeating Britain.

After the revolution, militias continued to defend their communities. They also defended against attacks by Native Americans. Sometimes they served as a police force.

Guns in the United States

Such militias no longer exist in the United States. Still, many Americans own guns. They base the right to own weapons on the Second Amendment.

Many Americans use their guns to hunt. Others collect guns. Some use guns for personal safety. They may want to protect against intruders or attackers.

Buying and selling guns is a major business in the United States. Every year, approximately 8 million guns are made globally. Each year, 4.5 million are sold to Americans. Approximately 31 percent of American households own firearms.

National Rifle Association

The National Rifle Association (NRA) was founded in 1871. It promotes gun safety and education. It is also a powerful lobbying group. It strongly opposes restrictions on guns. The NRA's goal is to expand Second Amendment rights. The group has blocked many gun control bills from becoming law.

Gun Control

Many gun owners are responsible. They have permits and training. They keep their guns safely away from children. Still, gun users kill approximately 33,000 people each year in the United States.

Federal law restricts gun ownership in some ways. Some people cannot own guns. They include criminals and people with mental illnesses. Gun laws have created waiting periods. Some states require buyers to wait five days before they can take home a weapon. The government runs a background check while they wait.

Mass shootings have kept the issue of gun control in the news. Many Americans favor gun control laws. A majority of gun owners support background checks. Other Americans argue strongly against all restrictions on guns. They worry that new laws could take away their Second Amendment rights.

EXPLORE ONLINE

The Second Amendment has a rich history. Laws often change over time. The right to bear arms has been extended and limited in many ways. Visit the website below to learn more about the Second Amendment. What new information did you find on this website?

History of the Second Amendment
mycorelibrary.com/constitutional-rights

CHAPTER FOUR

RIGHT TO PRIVACY

The Fourth Amendment protects Americans against "unreasonable searches and seizures." This means the government needs a warrant to search someone's property. A warrant is a document. It gives police permission to search. The police ask judges for search warrants. They explain why they think they will find evidence of a crime. The police must show a

Los Angeles police arrive with a warrant to search the home of a crime suspect.

good reason. Otherwise a judge will not allow it. Search warrants cannot be issued without cause. The warrant details what the police can search. It also details what kind of evidence they can take.

Privacy in the Digital Age

The Founding Fathers wrote the Fourth Amendment to protect people's privacy. Today's technology makes it difficult to know how to interpret it. People spend a lot of their time on the Internet. They share messages, photos, and videos. Are Facebook posts considered private information? What about posts shared with friends?

Boston lawyer Louis D. Brandeis lived long before the digital age. But Brandeis foresaw how new devices might threaten personal privacy. In 1890 he coauthored an important article. It was called "The Right to Privacy." The article appeared in the *Harvard Law Review*. He argued for the right "to be let alone" in the article. Brandeis also gave his opinion on privacy in a famous case. *Olmstead v. United States* involved illegal wiretapping by the government.

Olmstead v. United States

Seattle police officer Roy Olmstead began illegally selling alcohol in the 1920s. This was during a time in American history called Prohibition. Prohibition made it against the law to sell alcohol. The government decided to collect evidence against Olmstead. It wiretapped his telephone conversations. The evidence was used to convict Olmstead in 1926. He appealed. His lawyers argued the government violated Olmstead's right to privacy. The US Supreme Court let his conviction stand. It later reversed its decision on wiretaps. In 1935 Olmstead received a presidential pardon. But he had already served his sentence by then.

The Patriot Act

Congress approved the Patriot Act in 2001. Terrorists had attacked the country on September 11, 2001. The act gave the government more power to track and stop terrorists.

One section allowed "roving wiretaps." This allowed the government to continue pursuing a suspect, even if he or she switched phones. Another section allowed "sneak and peek" warrants. They allowed police to secretly search a person's home or business without letting the individual know beforehand.

In 2001 many people supported the Patriot Act. They feared another attack. Today more people are critical of the law. They say that it violates civil liberties and the right to privacy. The US government is still learning how the Fourth Amendment will work in the digital age.

Legal scholars still refer to Louis Brandeis's 1890 article, "The Right to Privacy." Some call it one of the most important law articles in American history. Brandeis became a Supreme Court justice in 1916.

> *That the individual shall have full protection in person and in property is a principle as old as the common law. . . . [But] recent inventions and business methods call attention to the next step which must be taken for the protection of the person, and for securing to the individual . . . the right "to be let alone." Instantaneous photographs and newspaper enterprise have invaded the sacred precincts of private and domestic life; and numerous mechanical devices threaten to make good the prediction that "what is whispered in the closet shall be proclaimed from the house-tops."*

Source: Leah Burrows. "To Be Let Alone: Brandeis Foresaw Privacy Problems." BrandeisNow. Brandeis University, July 24, 2013. Web. Accessed January 31, 2016.

What's the Big Idea?

Read this passage carefully. What is its main idea? Name a few details that support this main idea.

CHAPTER FIVE

RIGHTS IN COURT

The Founding Fathers had seen how oppressive Britain's government was. Citizens could be unjustly arrested. People had little hope of being released. Amendments Five, Six, Seven, and Eight protect accused people. They help ensure that justice is served.

A protester in Washington, DC, is handcuffed by police.

The Miranda Warning

In 1963 police questioned Ernesto Miranda for two hours. He did not ask for a lawyer. He confessed to the crime. Later a lawyer for Miranda appealed. He argued that Miranda's confession was false and coerced. The US Supreme Court heard the case. The justices ruled that US citizens must be read their rights before questioning. Miranda was acquitted. This decision led to the Miranda warning. Police must read this statement. It informs a person of his or her legal rights.

Due Process of Law

Due process is central to the Bill of Rights. It means the government must treat accused people fairly. The Fifth Amendment says that people cannot be forced to confess. It also prevents a person from being charged with the same crime twice. This is known as double jeopardy. If a person is found not guilty, that is the end of the case against them. This stops them from being unfairly targeted. Even if new evidence is discovered, he or she cannot be charged again.

On Trial

The Sixth Amendment guarantees the right to a public trial. When a person is arrested, he or she is accused of a crime. The person is not guilty yet. Guilt is decided in court. The Sixth Amendment helps ensure a fair trial. Trials must be judged by a jury of peers. The accused have the right to a lawyer. They also have the right to confront their accusers in court.

Jury Duty

Serving on a jury is a responsibility of American citizens. Potential jurors are picked randomly from the community. Lawyers from both sides help chose which jurors will serve on the case. They want people who can be unbiased. Accused people have the right to a trial by jury. The jury listens to the case and they discuss the facts. They decide whether the accused person is guilty.

Cruel and Unusual Punishment

The death penalty is the harshest punishment for a crime. It is reserved only for very serious crimes, such as murder. The death penalty has been outlawed in

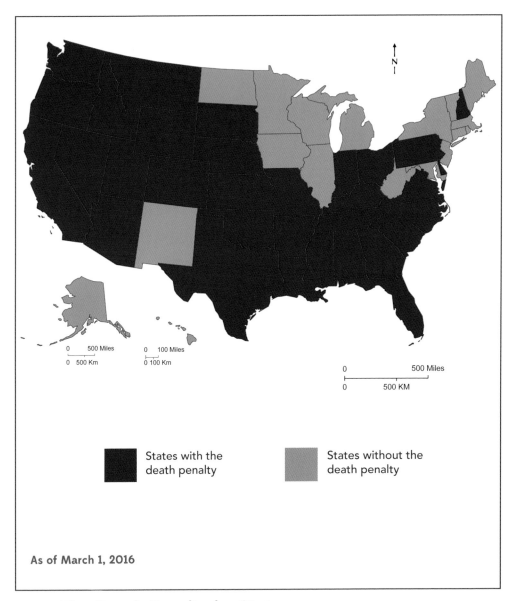

As of March 1, 2016

The Death Penalty by State

The death penalty is controversial. It is still used in the United States, though. Thirty-two states currently have the death penalty. Eighteen states and the District of Columbia do not. Does your state have the death penalty? Which regions of the country favor the death penalty? Which regions do not?

Bail bonds companies help people put up money for bail. If the person does not return to court, the bail bonds company may be allowed to arrest and bring the person to court.

some states. Many people say it violates the Eighth Amendment.

The Eighth Amendment bans cruel and unusual punishment. But it does not describe what punishments this includes. Courts play a big role in interpreting this.

The Eighth Amendment limits bail too. Bail is money that a person can pay to be released until his or her trial. Judges may set bail high enough to make sure the person will return to court for the trial.

CHAPTER SIX

CIVIL RIGHTS

The Bill of Rights did not give rights to all Americans. For many years, its rights applied only to white men. Women, African Americans, and Native Americans waited decades to gain equal rights.

Most African Americans were enslaved when the US Constitution was written. Slave codes governed them. These codes denied them the right to go to

At the August 1963 March on Washington, protesters called for protecting the civil rights of African Americans.

PERSPECTIVES

Birthright Citizenship

The Fourteenth Amendment says all people born or naturalized in the United States are citizens. Congress drafted the amendment with former slaves in mind. Representatives wanted them to have civil rights. Today, some people think this wording allows too many people to become citizens. Mothers who are not citizens may give birth in the United States. Their children then become US citizens. Senator Lindsey Graham opposes this. He said, "Birthright citizenship I think is a mistake. We should change our Constitution." The idea of changing the amendment has gained some popularity.

court. They could not create contracts or own property. They could not own guns or meet in groups.

In 1857 the Supreme Court even ruled they were not citizens. Chief Justice Roger Taney wrote that African Americans "had no rights which the white man was bound to respect."

This legal view did not change until the Thirteenth Amendment. It took effect after the American Civil War (1861–1865). The Thirteenth Amendment made slavery illegal. Soon after came the Fourteenth Amendment in 1868. The Fifteenth Amendment followed in 1870. These gave all men born in the United States full citizenship and the right to vote.

State lawmakers began passing laws to get around these amendments. They became known as Jim Crow laws. This system of segregation lasted from the 1880s to the mid-1960s. It took place mainly in the southern United States. Jim Crow laws made it difficult or impossible for African Americans to vote. The Voting Rights Act outlawed this practice. It passed in 1965.

The Constitution and Native Americans

The US Constitution did not apply to Native Americans when it was drafted. Native Americans lived within US borders. But they had their own separate nations. They did not have any rights under US law. On June 2, 1924, Congress finally granted citizenship to Native Americans.

Rights for Women

It took until 1920 for women to gain the right to vote. In that year, the Nineteenth Amendment passed. It made voting legal for women. Shortly after, an Equal Rights Amendment (ERA) was proposed. It would guarantee equality for women. The ERA was introduced in 1923. It failed to pass. Each year, the ERA was proposed to Congress. It did not pass until 1972. Even then it needed to be ratified by the states. Not enough states supported it, though. Gender equality is still not protected by the US Constitution.

Civil Liberties Then and Now

Constitutional rights are sometimes taken for granted. But the nation's Founding Fathers debated for months when drafting them. It was not an easy or quick process. The Bill of Rights they adopted more than 200 years ago describes some of Americans' most basic freedoms. It also spells out protections against a powerful central government. These rights are pillars of American democracy.

Equal Rights Amendment Map

Congress passed the Equal Rights Amendment in 1972. It needed to be ratified by the states. Supporters had until March 1979 to get three-quarters of the states to approve the ERA. The deadline was extended until 1982. It still failed to get the needed support. Do you believe the Constitution should be amended to include the Equal Rights Amendment? Why or why not?

FAST FACTS

- Delegates from 12 states met for the Constitutional Convention in the summer of 1787.
- Anti-Federalists criticized the Constitution and its strong central government. They believed states needed more control.
- The first ten amendments to the US Constitution are the Bill of Rights. These rights guarantee Americans basic rights and freedoms.
- The Bill of Rights did not originally apply to African Americans, women, or Native Americans.
- Freedom of religion, speech, and of the press are granted in the First Amendment.
- Today, one in three Americans owns a gun. Most guns are kept for personal safety, hunting, or for sport and recreation.
- Police may not search your property without good cause. They need a search warrant that explains what they want to search and where they want to look.
- Amendments Five through Eight protect people when they are accused of a crime by guaranteeing due process.

- The right to a fair and speedy trial, judged by a jury of peers, is detailed in the Sixth Amendment.
- The Thirteenth, Fourteenth, and Fifteenth Amendments gave African Americans equal rights under the Constitution.
- Women gained the right to vote with the Nineteenth Amendment. They are not specifically guaranteed equal rights under the Constitution.

STOP AND THINK

Why Do I Care?

Many Amendments expanding civil rights were passed years ago. You were not alive when these changes occurred, but the laws are still relevant to you. How do civil rights amendments affect your life? Are they still necessary today? Why or why not? Do you think new civil rights amendments are necessary to protect other Americans?

Dig Deeper

Chapter Two explains how free speech is denied through censorship. Books and other materials may be banned from schools and public libraries. Explore the titles of some banned books. How many have you heard of? Which ones have you read? See whether your library offers these titles. Explain why you think some of these titles may have been banned.

Tell the Tale

Chapter Five describes a person's rights when stopped by a police officer. Imagine you are a police officer and you have stopped a suspicious person. Write 200 words describing this scene. How do you make sure you are respecting the person's constitutional rights?

Say What?

Studying the Constitution can mean learning a lot of new vocabulary. Find five words in this book you have never heard before. Use a dictionary to find out what they mean. Then write the meanings in your own words. Use each word in a new sentence.

GLOSSARY

amendments
a change or an addition to a document

censorship
a system of suppressing material in books, movies, and other media

civil rights
the rights of people to enjoy freedom and equality

coerce
to pressure or force someone to do something

lobbying
swaying a public official to make decisions that benefit a particular cause

persecution
treating someone unfairly because of his or her race or religious or political beliefs

ratify
to make something official by signing or voting for it

rights
something that a person is or should be morally or legally allowed to have, get, or do

wiretap
to place a device on a telephone to secretly listen to private conversations

LEARN MORE

Books

Freedman, Russell. *In Defense of Liberty: The Story of America's Bill of Rights.* New York: Holiday House, 2003.

Haynes, Charles C. *First Freedoms: A Documentary History of First Amendment Rights in America.* New York: Oxford University Press, 2006.

Krull, Kathleen. *A Kid's Guide to America's Bill of Rights.* New York: HarperCollins, 2015.

Websites

To learn more about American Citizenship, visit **booklinks.abdopublishing.com**. These links are routinely monitored and updated to provide the most current information available.

Visit **mycorelibrary.com** for free additional tools for teachers and students.

INDEX

ABOUT THE AUTHOR

Jill Sherman lives and writes in Brooklyn, New York. She has written over a dozen books for young people. She enjoys researching new topics and is thrilled to be sharing the meaning of the American experience with young readers.